SAVED LIVING and FORGIVEN

Spiritual Prayers and Practices to Help You Take the Lord with You Everywhere You Go

LAMONT HILL

Copyright © 2020 by Lamont Hill

All rights reserved. No part of this book may be reproduced in any form by any electronic or mechanical means, including photocopying, recording, or information storage and retrieval without permission in writing from the author.

ISBN-13: 978-0-578-79482-2

Printed in the U.S.A.

Editing: Daria Anne DiGiovanni

Cover Design: Zeljka Kojic

Table of Contents

Introduction 1
FOOD FOR THOUGHT 3
   Chapter 1 – WORDS OF INSPIRATION 5
   Chapter 2 – WORDS OF ENCOURAGEMENT 9
   Chapter 3 – READ YOUR BIBLE 13
   Chapter 4 – HIS MERCY ENDURES FOREVER 15
PRAYER 19
   Chapter 5 – THINGS THAT DELAY PRAYERS 21
   Chapter 6 – HOW FAR AWAY IS GOD? 23
   Chapter 7 – PRAYER OF FAITH 25
   Chapter 8 – I AM YOURS 27
   Chapter 9 – PSALMS SCRIPTURE PRAYER 29
FAITH 31
   Chapter 10 – REAL TALK 33
   Chapter 11 – WALK THE GOOD WALK OF FAITH 39
   Chapter 12 – I SURRENDER 41
   Chapter 13 – THE GIFT OF RIGHTEOUSNESS 45
   Chapter 14 – WHO ARE YOU IN CHRIST? 49
OBEDIENCE 53
   Chapter 15 – SEEK THE LORD 55
   Chapter 16 – GOD'S LOVE 57
   Chapter 17 – CONSUMMATE YOUR LOVE FOR GOD 59

Chapter 18 – FORGIVENESS 61

SALVATION AND DEVOTION **63**

Chapter 19 – CONFESSION 65

Chapter 20 – BE COMPLETE 67

Chapter 21 – REVEALING THOUGHTS 69

Chapter 22 – PLANT YOUR SEED 71

Chapter 23 – CONSCIENCE CHECK 73

COMMITMENT **75**

Chapter 24 – A LISTENING EAR BECOMES AN OBEDIENT HEART 77

Chapter 25 – TRANSFORMED INTO THE LIGHT 81

Chapter 26 – PURIFIED IN THE LIGHT 83

Chapter 27 – CLOSING THOUGHTS AND PRAYER 87

ABOUT THE AUTHOR **91**

REFERENCES **93**

MY JOURNEY WITH THE LORD **95**

NOTES TO HELP YOU STAY CONNECTED 95

Dedication

To the memory of my parents: Thomas Sr. and Minnie Hill. I could never have done this without your faith, support, and constant encouragement. Thank you for teaching me to believe in God, in myself, and my dreams.

To my wife and best friend: Shirley. I affectionately dedicate this to you. Sharing our life and love along this journey is a blessing beyond words. Thanks for all the times you listened and helped me through this process.

To my children: Pamela, Jason, Khandis, Gwen, and Ariel: You are my shining stars and future generations. Thanks for always being an inspiration to me.

Introduction

First, and foremost I give thanks to God, our Creator, who inspired me to write and reflect on His Holy scriptures. All the glory and praise belong to the Father of Light; nothing would be possible without Him. Thank you, Lord God.

Saved, Living, and Forgiven is a book of spiritual prayers and thoughts reflecting on Jehovah God and Lord Jesus Christ. I based it on scriptures that show us how we should conduct ourselves as servants and children of God. The positive reinforcement to be a doer of His word. Use it as a training tool and a daily reminder that God is always present. He is there waiting to open doors that need to be opened while closing doors that need to be closed. I believe, trust, and depend on the Word; the Holy Spirit leads us as we walk with the authority and power given to us.

I am saved because I know Jesus Christ is the Son of God, and He laid down His life for my sins at Calvary, then rose on the third day. I am living because I walk in the Word, imitating Jesus's righteousness to be his disciple. I am forgiven because Jesus redeemed us back to the Father, and God covers our carnal body with His grace, mercy, and favor as we seek to worship Him in spirit and truth. Therefore, we are saved, living, and forgiven of all our sins as we seek to live a righteous life. My prayer and goal are for you to receive God's message with all its revelations to enhance your spiritual experience walking in the light.

FOOD FOR THOUGHT

What Do You Desire?

Chapter 1

WORDS OF INSPIRATION

Time alone with God.

Find a time and place where you are free from all distractions and make it the biggest priority in your life to get there daily. God blesses each of us in different ways, and there is not a specific way His anointing covers us. For example, I am not great at remembering every scripture, chapter, and verse; but I know how to apply the scriptures to my life. Which is more important? The key is to receive the Word and apply it to your everyday existence. Some folks may think that knowing scriptures is more critical but being a servant of the Lord means to serve the needs of the lost, no matter the sacrifice. Therefore, it is crucial to possess *both* knowledge of Scriptural truth and an ability to apply it.

As Christians, we must always realize none of us have arrived; it is a constant reading and studying cycle. Each time I read different chapters in the Bible I gain a new understanding of the Word. I call it spiritual growth in Christ. ISAIAH 41:10 NKJV says, "Fear not, for I am with you; be not anxious, I am your God. I will strengthen you, yes I will help you, I will uphold you with My righteous right hand."

Signs and wonders — Moses, a servant of God, trusted Him and obeyed His commands. The Israelites crossed the Red Sea on dry ground, but Pharaoh's army drowned in it. Although there have been countless plagues upon the earth, Our God has brought us through to the other side. Remain faithful and watch the goodness of the Lord shine on your life. Lift your voice to God in your meditation; He will preserve your life from the fear of the enemy.

How blessed we became when the people cried out for Jesus to be crucified, "His blood be on us and our children," MATTHEW 27:25 NKJV. The powerful blood of Jesus covers us and washes our sins away. Thank you, Jesus, for laying your life down for us.

Some people never seem to acknowledge the Lord until something tragic happens, such as the death of a loved one or a dire health diagnosis. Do not be a "shelf worshipper." What do I mean by that? A shelf-worshipper only praises Jesus when they are in trouble, and then after the situation resolves, they put Jesus on the shelf until the next time they are in need. This practice is the worst-case scenario. Everyday, give thanks to the Lord our God and Savior. Acknowledge His presence for everything in your life, the good or the bad, and be a true worshipper whose faith is unwavering. Keep the line of communication open. Think of it this way: if you are in a bad situation and call on the name of Jesus, whose prayers and requests will He attend to first -- the one who is continuously in contact with Him or the person who only calls on him when they're in trouble? We all know that answer; straddling the fence is a dangerous place for your faith. Choose to serve the God of all creation and be on His team — the winning team.

Return to the Lord; all the power belongs to God. Stop fighting yourselves, surrender to his will, listen, and obey His commands. JEREMIAH 3:14-15 NKJV says, "Return to me you, backsliding children, for I am married to you. I will give you shepherds according to my heart that will feed you with knowledge and understanding." Are you listening? These are God's words proclaiming His love for us, printed in black and white for all to see. God wants all of us to return to Him, change our attitude, commit our hearts, and connect with Him, our Father. In JOHN 14:20-21 NKJV, Jesus states, "At that day you will know that I am in the Father and you are in Me, and I am in you. He who has My commandments and keeps them is the one who loves Me, and whoever loves Me will be loved by my Father, and I will love him and reveal Myself to him."

Playtime is over: let us get serious in giving our Lord His just due. We must offer all our worship and praise to glorify His Holy name, repent of your sins, and be washed clean. Come into the marvelous light, beloved people of God, before it is too late. These are words of inspiration to apply to your life today. Amen.

Chapter 2

WORDS OF ENCOURAGEMENT

I do not want to be the person I once was. I renew my mind daily to slay my old self, so I can now walk in the light and spiritual rebirth of our Creator who loved me from the beginning of time. The beauty of God's word is that it always prevails. We must keep His Word in our mouth, speak it into the atmosphere, and engrave His words in our hearts. The world offers hardship and pain, then more suffering; however, God promises rest for those who believe in Him. "The eye of the Lord is on those who fear Him, on those who hope in His mercy to deliver their soul from death and to keep them alive in famine," PSALMS 33:18-19 NKJV.

Whose heart is larger than our God Lord Jesus? If you do not know — no one! All who are the Lord's He will not lose; no one can take us out of His hands. How good is God? Words cannot describe how wonderful and magnificent He is. His love is unconditional.

During a conversation with Elder Mary Dalton about the greatest love of all, she told me that every time you pick up your Bible to read it, Jesus says, "I love you." If you think about it, this is a profound statement. It is like Jesus saying, "I love you, abide in me, and I will abide in you." Live your life to be worthy and hope in the mercy, peace, and loving-kindness of our God. We are valuable to God; we have a purpose of being whole, having faith that our God is the greatest love of all and lives inside of us in the form of the Holy Spirit.

Elder Opal Scales once said, "Satan is angry with God because our Lord forgives us for our sins, but He will not forgive him. So, therefore Satan is trying to take as many of us as possible to hell with him. We must be the church. Let God's light shine from you; when you walk into a room, let them see the presence of Jesus."

We must attempt to save the lost at any cost, be committed, and do not quit. PROVERBS 2:10-11 NKJV tells us, "When wisdom enters your heart and knowledge is pleasant to your soul, discretion will preserve you, understanding will keep you." You have the victory in Jesus. Be vigilant because you do not know the time or the hour the Lord will return. Have your house in order. Your soul belongs to God. Do not fall asleep; be a doer of the Word and listen to the voice of God.

My co-laborer, James Davis, spoke about the power of prayer: when we talk about prayer, people often shy away from the topic because they believe they do not know what to say to God. I know how that feels. There was a time when I would not pray in front of people, or I would compare myself to others, believing that my prayers did not matter because I was not as eloquent as the person praying before me. It was a trick of the enemy to suppress my relationship with God. I determined within my heart that I would no longer allow fear to stop me from praying. The key was to understand what prayer was truly all about.

So, what is prayer?

Prayer is a conversation with God. In prayer, you build a relationship of trust and love with God. Just as there is no magic formula in your conversation with friends, bosses, or loved ones, there is no magic formula to prayer. Why would you try to be all complex with God? Yes, He knows our thoughts even before we utter them, but God truly desires to hear from our hearts. The supplication, the hurt, the pain, the disappointments, the needs, the wants, and on and on. Just like your best friend, God wants to hear it all. When you consider someone your best friend, you talk to them continually, which is a relationship. What I have described is an excellent illustration of prayer. We must be in a constant connection with God. COLOSSIANS

4:2 AMP implores, "Be persistent and devoted to prayer, being alert and focused on your prayer life with an attitude of thanksgiving."

Align your heart and pray that you will be seated on the right side of God. Let His words to you be, "Well done, my good and faithful servant." We know without the Holy Spirit, no one can be ready for the coming of Jesus. You must be on point, do not miss your blessing because you failed to prepare. Speak in a manner that will edify one another. Do not be like immature children in your understanding; however, just like an innocent baby, show no malice toward anyone. Let us not fight against God but *for* God. When God cleanses us, we will be made whole. "The Lord has given me the tongue of the learned that I should know how to speak a word in season to him who is weary He awakens my ears to hear as the learned," ISAIAH 50:4 NKJV.

I realize and understand that we need God more than we need anything else. Think of all the ways we pray and worship. Use that power our Father gives us, open your mouth, and speak your destiny into existence; never doubt the power of His revelation. PSALMS 34:19,22 NKJV tells us, "Many are the afflictions of the righteous, but the Lord delivers us out of them all. The Lord redeems the souls of His servants, and none of those who trust in Him shall be condemned."

We must go through many tribulations in life to enter the kingdom of God, but our trials are nothing compared to what happened to Jesus. The chief priest threw Jesus in jail; they beat, tortured, and mocked Him. Jesus hanged on a tree and died for the sins of the entire world. "Yet it pleased the Lord to bruise Him; he had put him to grief when God made his soul an offering for sin. He shall see His seed; He shall prolong His days, and the pleasure of the Lord shall prosper in His hand," ISAIAH 53:10 NKJV. Three days He laid in a tomb; on Sunday morning, He rose with all power in his hand. Praise God, thank you, Jesus. Rest in God's voice and claim His unconditional love, the greatest love of all time, our Savior Jesus Christ.

It is essential to stay connected, make good use of your prayer closet, and give your honor, integrity, faith, and trust to the Lord. Amen.

Chapter 3

READ YOUR BIBLE

"To do righteousness and justice is more acceptable to the Lord than sacrifice," PROVERBS 21:3 NKJV.

"The light of the eyes rejoices the heart, and a good report makes the bones healthy," PROVERBS 15:30 NKJV.

You have not obeyed the voice of the Lord your God or anyone He has sent to you. Why is it so hard for us to be obedient and righteous? According to JOSHUA 1:8 NKJV, "The Book of the Law shall not depart from your mouth; you shall meditate in it day and night that you may observe to do according to all that is written in it. For then, you will make your ways prosperous, and then, you will have good success."

How good and pleasant it is for all the brethren to dwell together in unity. With wisdom, a house is built, and through understanding, it is established. We must have a new spirit and walk in a new life, based on our faith in the Lord our God, that He may show us how we shall walk and the things we should do. In PSALM 132, God said, "I will prepare a lamp for My Anointed, his enemies I will clothe with shame. But upon him, his crown shall flourish."

Do you understand what God promises us?

Take the Lord with you everywhere you go; read your Bible. God wants us to have the kingdom and everything that goes with it. Frank Turner Jr. noted, "A word is a medium by which thoughts are expressed; therefore, the Bible is the mind of God on a printed page He has given us to renew our thinking. As you feed yourself on the Word of God and absorb it into your heart, you will nurture your made-up mind into a renewed mind and experience the power of a changed mind."

Beloved, everything you need is in the pages of the Bible. Give God some of your time, open the Book of Life, and read what the Lord is telling you. Do not think or feel you are not worthy. Jesus died and rose on the third day just to give you a chance to repent and turn your life around. God is love, and He loves you. He wants to be a friend to you. I do not know about you, but I need the Lord 24-7. I cannot function without him guiding me through the storms in my life and making my path clear. I want to be wherever God is.

Will there be pain and hardship along the way?

Yes. Many are the afflictions of the righteous, but the Lord will see you through. 2 TIMOTHY 2:15 NKJV reads, "Be diligent to present yourself approved to God; a worker who does not need to be ashamed, rightly dividing the word of truth." Beloved, read your Bible and find the truth for yourselves. Fight your battles on your knees and give them to the Lord, for there is nothing too hard for Him. My Brothers and Sisters never stop praying; it is your power and spiritual connection to our Creator, the Most High God. The Book of Life, your Bible, contains the solution to every problem: how you should live, be blessed, and bless someone else. May God's peace reign over your life. Amen.

Chapter 4

HIS MERCY ENDURES FOREVER

The dictionary defines mercy as "compassion or forbearance (patience) to an offender or one subject to one's power; a blessing that is an act of divine favor or compassionate treatment of those in distress; a kind, gentle treatment, especially towards someone undeserving of it."

It defines the word understanding as "the mental process of a person who comprehends; a knowledge of or familiarity with a thing; a skill in dealing with or handling something; and the capacity for sharing the feeling of another."

HEBREWS 4:12 NKJV tells us, "For the word of God is living and powerful and is sharper than any two-edged sword, piercing even to the division of soul and spirit, and of joints and marrow and is a discerner of the thoughts and intents of the heart." When we speak of God's attributes, we are talking about those characteristics that help us understand who He truly is. Having been justified by His grace, we have become heirs according to the hope of eternal life. Whoever finds God finds life and obtains favor from the Lord; His love covers all sin. The Lord shall preserve you going out and you coming in from this time forth to forever. Our help is in the name of the Lord, who made heaven and earth.

As for God, His ways are perfect, and his words are proven. He is a shield to all who trust in Him. Those who trust in the Lord are like Mount Zion, which cannot be moved; it remains forever. A man or woman with understanding walks in righteousness, they think before they speak, and they keep a tempered spirit that will always be able to hear and know His voice.

Lips that speak Truth will be established forever, but a lying tongue is but for a moment. Those who deal truthfully are God's delight. The name of the

Lord is a strong tower and all the righteous run to it for safety. HEBREWS 6:10 NKJV teaches, "For God is not unjust to forget your works and labor of love which you have shown to His name; *in that,* you have ministered to the Saints, and do minister." God will be your mouth and teach you the words you shall say and do. His mercy endures forever.

To we the believers, it has been granted on behalf of Christ to suffer for His sake. Everything has its time and season; search me, God, you know my heart, lead me in the way of your everlasting love. By faith, we understand who we are in Christ, the children of promise. His mercy endures forever. Our sins' confession to a loving and forgiving GOD removes our burden and gives us a renewed sense of joy. All of us were born spiritually blind until God heals our blindness -- until then, we will not see and appreciate the spiritual truth. Let your heart be loyal to the Lord, our God. The key is to talk to God and Jesus, who is an intercessor on our behalf. The Lord is good, and His tender mercies are over all His work.

Sin is the cause of all the misery in the world. When we sin against God, we cannot hide; there are consequences to pay. Every day our flesh engages in constant warfare with our spirit. We are sick and need God's help because we do not get it right all the time, and we fall short. Even though we want to be obedient, sometimes, we are disobedient. The one thing we have is a loving and forgiving Father. Lord, you know what a temptation to us will be; teach us to walk away from anything ungodly or unrighteous. Keep us rooted and grounded in your love.

We do not know what any day may bring. We must be patient until the coming of the Lord. Let the truth rest in your spirit and on your lips. Remember those who have spoken the word of God to you, whose faith is the outcome of their conduct. We live the Word by walking in the Word. Always take the Lord with you everywhere you go.

By walking in God's will, we connect our lifeline to trust and faith in God's covenant with an understanding of God's Word. Faith is the essential key to open the door so God can come in. The only way He will respond to us if we believe in Jesus Christ His Son. Jesus' blood purifies our sins; no one can come to the Father except through Jesus the light of the world. We have the favor, blessing, anointing, and the promises of God. His mercies endure forever.

Let us talk about the mercies of God. Did you know when we sin, we are putting generational curses on our children? Both the Old and New Testaments in the Bible instruct us how to live. We cannot just take the parts we like; we must absorb it all. The Bible is a book of love, mercy, and forgiveness. The result? Our merciful and loving God wants us to want him, much like voting for a president. God wants us to choose Him just like He has chosen us; He will never force us because He gave us free will to make our own decisions.

However, if you trust Him and follow His commandments, the Lord will bless you. He will cover you and your children's children if you walk in His law. His mercy does endure forever, and we must be grateful and give Him honor and glory for His goodness. Frances Taylor Gench said, "Love demands a response, and the greater the love, the greater our desire to be equal to that love. With Christ, there is no way for our love to be equal to His." All we can do is follow Jesus to the best of our ability and to love others as He loved us. We were not redeemed with corruptible things like silver or gold but with the precious blood of Christ. Amen.

PRAYER

Fight Your Battles On Your Knees

Chapter 5

THINGS THAT DELAY PRAYERS

Sometimes God delays His answers to our prayers for many different reasons:

1) The timing is not right. However, God may answer it later.

2) God wants you to clarify the request so that when the answer comes, you can recognize it. Often, we do not even acknowledge that God has answered a prayer request because we did not crystallize it sufficiently in our minds.

3) God might delay the answer to create a sense of expectation and call attention to the fact that it was Him who answered -- not good luck or natural consequences.

4) God is giving us time to repent of our sins.

5) God wants to draw us into a deeper relationship with Him. When things come too easy, we tend to take it for granted, but God wants us to pray with intention. Therefore, the answers do not come easily.

When we fear that God is not answering our prayer for no discernable reason, the cause for the delay could be one or more of the five reasons I outlined above. A prayerful life is a form of discipline – when you wake up, put on your Helmet of Salvation and Full Armor of God. When you open your eyes, praise God, and thank Him for all He has given you and done for you. Be humble, submit, and surrender yourself before the throne of Christ to walk upright and let your light shine. Keep peace in your heart; do not allow others to provoke you into arguments or stoke your anger. Instead, bless them, smile, and go in peace.

Pray for everyone, including those who mistreat you. Be of good cheer; be happy because Jesus is the strength of your joy. Read your Bible and fill up your spiritual tank. Through prayer, receive your knowledge and understanding of the power of God. Pray for enlightenment about the things you do not understand, and ask God, in Jesus' name, to reveal them to you so that you can understand.

Praise time is all the time. Take the Lord with you everywhere you go. Praise Him in the morning when you wake up and let God walk with you all day. Sing praises in your heart, glorify, always lift the Lord up. Let the Lord know that he is worthy to be praised by saying it. Raise your hands and bless His name day and night. Confess, praise, glorify, and believe what you affirm in prayer; then act as if you have already received it. Amen.

Chapter 6

HOW FAR AWAY IS GOD?

God is just one prayer away! Right when you talk to God, you are praying in the spiritual realm. All things are seen and unseen; God is closer than we sometimes realize when we use written scriptures. He releases His angels to encamp around us to protect and minister to us.

Prayerless people cut themselves off from God's prevailing power. The frequent result is the familiar feeling of being overwhelmed, beaten down, pushed around, and defeated. A great majority of people are willing to settle for lives like that, but you do not have to be one of them. Nobody should live like that. Prayer is the key to unlocking God's omnipotence in your life. When you develop a daily habit of prayer, you must maintain a regular prayer routine to stay connected to God and avoid becoming spiritually unbalanced.

How do you speak a prayer so filled with faith that it can move a mountain? By believing it is done without any doubt in your mind, moving forward in obedience as you walk with God. As your faith grows, your confidence in His word will increase, and your prayers will have power. Focus your attention on God, His glory, and omnipotence, then follow His lead as you walk in faith, remove all distractions, and watch Him move mountains for you. Strength comes out of solitude, the time you intentionally reserve for quality prayer time, not "leftover" time after you've tended to everything else in your life. Set aside time each day to contemplate, meditate, and reflect on the written word of God.

You must know in your heart that He is there to lift you up! Lay all your burdens down and submit yourself to the power of the Almighty. We need to pray to make it through the day. When you engage in sincere prayer, humble yourself, surrender to the will of God, and yield your heart to Him,

He will give you peace of mind. When you cast your worries on the Lord, our Father will send the Comforter, the Holy Spirit, to comfort and carry you, if necessary. Remember, you are blessed and highly favored!

Chapter 7

PRAYER OF FAITH

In PROVERBS 3:27 NKJV, we read, "Do not withhold good from those to whom it is due when it is in the power of your hand to do so." Seek the word of God at all times. All who desire to live godly in Christ will suffer persecution, but every word of God is pure, and He is a shield to those who put their trust in Him. Turn my eyes from looking at worthless things and revive me in your ways. Strengthen me according to your word, Lord. Remove from me the path of lying I have chosen over the path of truth. I have been crucified with Christ. It is no longer I who live, but Christ lives in me. The life I now live in the flesh I live by faith, by faith in the Son of God who loved me and gave himself for me. My faith is not in the wisdom of men but the omnipotence of God. My life is continually in your hands, Lord, and I have not forgotten your law. Cast away from me all the transgressions which I have committed Lord, give me a new heart and spirit. Blessed are You O Lord, teach me your statutes, deal bountifully with your servant so I may live and have your peace, and live with joy in your word. I lift your name and glorify your presence in my life. I love you, Lord, and I need you. In Jesus' name, I praise you, and thank you. Amen.

Chapter 8

I AM YOURS

Thank you, Father God, for all you do for me. I am profoundly grateful that you chose me, with all my flaws and shortcomings. As a recipient of your grace and mercy, I gradually become aware of my value. I am not alone, Lord; you walk through the fire and valleys with me. You purge me and carry me when I am weak. Lord God, your unconditional love is beyond the understanding of my mind; but I give you thanks, and I praise your Holy Name for your goodness. Thank you, Father, for renewing my mind and giving me the confidence to completely trust in your words, and for your promises to whoever walks before you with a pure heart and clean hands.

I need you, Lord, to guide me and keep me on the path of righteousness. I love you, Lord. Please, God, never leave me uncovered from your saving grace. I belong to you, and the only place I want to be is in the high tower of your unfailing love. I submit and humble my soul for deliverance and salvation. I close this prayer with thanksgiving and praise to your Holy Name, Father, through Jesus Christ. Amen.

Chapter 9

PSALMS SCRIPTURE PRAYER

Psalms 25- Psalms 50

"Remember not the sins of my youth, nor my transgressions. According to Your mercy, remember only me for your goodness sake, O Lord. Good and upright is the Lord; therefore, he will teach sinners the way. Whoever offers praise glorifies Me, and to him that orders his conduct aright will I show the salvation of God. Hide your face from my sins and blot out all my iniquities. Create in me a clean heart, O God, and renew a right spirit within me. Restore unto me the joy of your salvation and uphold me with your free spirit. Mark the perfect man and behold the upright, for the end of that man is peace. But the salvation of the righteous is of the Lord…He is their strength in time of trouble. For his anger endureth but a moment, in his favor is life…weeping may endure for a night, but joy comes in the morning. In you, O Lord, do I put my trust, let me never be ashamed: deliver me in your righteousness…You are my rock and my fortress; therefore, for Your name's sake, lead me and guide me. The Lord is my strength and my shield. My heart greatly rejoices, and with my song will I praise Him…the Lord is our strength, and He is the saving strength of his anointed. Save your people and bless Your inheritance. Feed them also and lift them up forever…give unto the Lord the glory due to His name. Worship the Lord in the beauty of holiness…show me your ways, O Lord, teach me your paths. Lead me in Your truth and teach me, for you are the God of my salvation…On You do I wait all the day long. Remember, O Lord, Your tender mercies and Your loving kindness, for they have been ever of old," PSALMS 25-50, NKJV.

All the glory to God, Amen, and Hallelujah! Thank you, Father. In Jesus' name, I pray, Amen.

FAITH

Believe in A Power Greater Than Yourself

Chapter 10

REAL TALK

Believing in the Bible is ultimately a matter of informed faith. You either believe what the word of God says about itself, or you do not. You either accept the testimony of Jesus Christ regarding the word of God, or you do not. Now let us consider the value of the words God provides to us in the Bible. Anyone who will take the time can see and understand what God has given us in His word and how it applies to us today.

No matter how much you know about God's word, the scriptures will never benefit your life if you do not apply what you learn. "To be a hearer of the word only and not a doer of the word is to deceive yourself," JAMES 1:22 NKJV. Therefore, the application is vital. Observation and interpretation are the "hearing" of God's word, and with the application, you will be transformed into Christ's image. Application is the embracing of truth, the "doing" of God's word; it is the process that allows God to work in our lives. When we spend time studying His word, God equips us through teaching, commands, promises, exhortation, and warnings. You must open your Bible and read it for yourself.

God reveals himself through His word; He shows us how to live. In MATTHEW 4:4 NKJV, Jesus made it clear, "Man shall not live by bread alone, but by every word that proceeds from the mouth of God." As you study the Bible with the help of the Holy Spirit and live out the truths that God reveals to you, you will discover new stability, strength, and confidence. Find the truth for yourself, discern what it means, and then apply it to your life.

Everything we do must line up with God's word and His laws; if not, it is a sin. We all have tribulations, ROMANS 5:3-5 NKJV says, "But we also glory in tribulations, knowing that tribulation produces perseverance; and perseverance, character; and character hope. Hope does not disappoint because the love of God has been poured out in our hearts by the Holy Spirit that was given to us." If we apply a kingdom mindset and walk into the situation with peace in our hearts, we will walk out with joy. A kingdom mindset means the spiritual reign of authority that a person is aware of concerning the presence of God and Jesus, of elevating our thoughts of God above doubt or contemplation of evil.

"We walk by faith not by sight; the just shall live by faith," 2 CORINTHIANS 5:7 NKJV. "We are confident if anyone is in Christ, he is a new creature; old things have passed away, and all things have become new," 2 CORINTHIANS 5:17 NKJV. Now all things are of God, who has reconciled us to Himself through Jesus, and He has given us the ministry of reconciliation. Redeem your time; we are the temple of the living God. In 2 CORINTHIANS 6:16 NKJV, God said, "I will dwell in them and walk among them, I will be their God, and they shall be my people." When you are baptized, you are baptized in the Father, the Son, and the Holy Spirit; so God dwells in you by the Holy Spirit.

We can come freely to God and give all our hearts to Him and lay down all our burdens. He hears you, and He is waiting for you to ask Him into your life. BELOVED, MAKE THE CALL! Call on the name of JESUS.

LUKE 17:20-21 NKJV tells us, "The kingdom of God does not come with observation nor will they say see here or see there; for indeed the kingdom of God is within you." The Holy Spirit lives in you. LUKE 10:19-20 NKJV declares, "I give you the authority to trample on serpents and scorpions, and overall the power of the enemy. Nothing shall by any means hurt you. Nevertheless, do not rejoice in this that the spirits are subject to you; but rather rejoice because your names are written in heaven."

We must speak life and our heart's desires into the atmosphere. ROMANS 8:31 NKJV says it best, "If God is for us, who can be against us?" Nothing or no one. Use the power God has given us to turn your situation around. We face warfare daily; we must resist the temptations of our flesh, submit to God's will, and let our spirit be in control. All our names are in the Book of Life; it is up to us to keep them there. We have the power, yet most of us do not use it. "Nothing shall be able to separate us from the love of God, which is in Christ Jesus our Lord," ROMANS 8:37 NKJV. The bread of God is He who came down from heaven and gives life to the world. Jesus is the bread of life.

Let us talk about our past: we all make mistakes, and sometimes it takes us a while to realize we made a mistake. So, what are we going to do about it? The critical point is to have a repenting heart; a repenting heart means you regret what has happened or what you have done and want to make an honest effort to resolve the problem. We can accomplish this by opening our mouths and using the power God has given us. Do not be ashamed to say, "I was wrong; I did not have any intentions to hurt or harm anyone." God will forgive you every time you ask. Caution: this does not mean you have a pass to keep repeating the same sin.

We all receive eternal life. The question is, do you want your eternal life to be in the company of God and Lord Jesus in heaven, where rivers of living water flow? There, you will be happy living in peace with the love of God. Or, will your eternal life be in hell with Satan and his demons, where you will suffer and burn in an unquenchable fire for eternity? All agony and pain -- no chance to redeem yourself. This is the naked truth we face. There is no sugar-coating it: *you* are the one who will choose.

God is not a grudge-holder. He makes a bad situation right; that is how much He loves us. God demonstrates His love toward us while we are still sinners. Christ died for us. Let us present our bodies as slaves of righteousness for holiness, having become slaves to God. You have fruited a harvest, and the end is everlasting life. With this promise, let us cleanse ourselves from all filthiness of our flesh and spirit, perfecting holiness in God.

Now is the time to return to God. Give your life to Him, and He will give you rest all around. It is an easy choice from my point of view. I want eternal peace and happiness -- not temporary happiness that is corruptible and does not last. Beloved, get your life back in line with our Father God, the Creator of all living things.

God calls us or refers to us in the Bible in four different ways. He calls us His children, His Sons and Daughters, and His people. What is the other name He calls us? We are His Saints.

I want to be a "Saint," not an "Aint." The difference between a Saint and an Aint is that a Saint gets back up when they fall off the path of righteousness, whereas an Aint just gives up and says, "Forget it, it is not going to matter." It does matter: our life is precious, and we are important to God. "Let every soul be subject to the higher powers; for there is no power but of God. The powers-that-be are ordained of God. The night is far spent, and the day is at hand; let us, therefore, cast off the works of darkness and put on the armor of light, Jesus Christ. We are children of light, not darkness," ROMANS 13 NKJV.

I urge you to reaffirm your love to be obedient in all things. Thanks be to God, who always leads us in victory in Jesus Christ.

2 CORINTHIANS 3:2-3 NKJV declares, "You are our epistle written in our hearts, known and read by all men; clearly, you are an epistle of Christ, ministered by us, written not with ink but by the Spirit of the living God, not on tablets of stone but on the tablets of flesh, *that is*, of the heart." AMEN. Translation: He is not only living in you; He is writing His laws in your heart. He is covering you and protecting you, and nothing and no

one can take you out of his hand. Do you love the Lord? If you love the Lord, say these words, "I surrender to You, Lord."

Beloved, it is time to do some soul-searching and decide whose team you want to join. Keep in mind tomorrow is not promised to anyone; man does not control time. There is no "do-over" in life; you have one life to get it right. Time is in God's hands; come to Jesus while you can. All hands-on-deck. Do not let your seat at Jesus' table in heaven be empty because you picked the wrong team. Amen.

Chapter 11

WALK THE GOOD WALK OF FAITH

Anchor yourself in the righteousness of God. Love your enemies, do good to them that hate you. Give the glory and praise to the Father, acknowledge his presence and power for all He does for you. "Bless them that curse you and pray for them which spitefully use you," LUKE 6:28 NKJV. It is a blessing to be a child of God; we should not be ashamed of Him, but rather, rejoice in the Lord. Greater is He that is in me than any man in the world. "Blessed is the nation whose God is Lord and the people He has chosen for His own inheritance," PSALMS 33:12 NKJV. Do not hold grudges, forgive those who abuse you, and return goodness for evil. We must bless others in our lives; I am not talking about your family only, but anyone in need that crosses your path. Have faith, believe that God will empower you with the things you need, give your money, time, service, and tithes to the Lord.

God is in the blessing business. When you give to God, He will give back to you. Help the stranger, give to the poor, and feed someone. You never know when you are in the company of an angel. Charity is the greatest gift, give your children to Jesus, and you give them eternal life; raise them properly, and they may leave, but they will come back to the righteousness of the Lord. Build yourself up with love, let your love shine…know and understand your gift, use it for the glory of God, and not to please man.

Are you submitting yourself and devoting your heart to God's word?

Untested faith is worthless to God. It is easy to praise God when everything is going well. In times of tribulation, pain, and hardship -- that is when the test comes. Overcome your obstacles, and walk around the wall, not into it. Keep giving God praise and endure to the end. Do not stop praising Him.

Crucify yourself daily with Jesus and walk in His righteousness. The foundation of God stands sure. Having this seal, the Lord knows all them that are His. Everyone that calls on the name of Christ departs from iniquity. Jesus is who we need! We must suffer sometimes; do not look back. Instead, strive toward the high calling of God and press toward the mark. Being a Christian is a profession. Just like any job you love, you try hard to learn about every possibility to ensure success. An athlete calls it being a student of the game. God's covenant is not a game, but you must study to learn how to be a professional at divining the word correctly. Disregard false teaching and doctrine. Anchor yourself in God's righteousness. Amen.

Chapter 12
I SURRENDER

I surrender my heart and mind to follow You. I submit my soul for your safekeeping, Lord. PROVERBS 7:1-2,4 NKJV commands, "Keep my words and treasure my commands within you. Keep my commands and live and my laws as the apple of your eyes. Say to wisdom, you are my sister and call understanding your nearest kin."

The Ark of the Covenant represents God's presence when we follow the commands. When we become aligned with God's words, life takes on a new meaning. You cannot fix what your faith will not face; faith must be beyond the facts. "Blessed is the man who walks not in the counsel of the ungodly, nor stands in the path of sinners, neither sits in the seat of the scornful," Psalm 1:1 NKJV.

The blessings of the Lord make one rich, and He adds no sorrow with it. Riches and honor come through humility and the fear of the Lord. There is no better time than now to have a heart-to-heart talk with God, so you can understand who you are in Christ Jesus. MATTHEW 7:21 NKJV warns, "Not everyone who says to me, 'Lord, Lord' shall enter the kingdom of heaven, but he who does the will of my Father in heaven." God has His hand all over you, protecting and anointing your spirit. Your Father's good pleasure is to give you the kingdom - a treasure in heaven that does not fail. "Where your treasure is, there your heart will be also," MATTHEW 6:21 NKJV.

Spiritual life begins with spiritual birth, which occurs through faith in Jesus Christ. Faith in Jesus infuses us with God's life – eternal life. PSALM 27:1 NKJV reminds us, "The Lord is my light and my salvation; Whom shall I fear? The Lord is the strength of my life; Of whom shall I be afraid?" Beloved, grow in the grace and knowledge of our Lord Jesus. Lord, show me the path of life with your presence, fulfill my joy. Lord, your word says in

PSALM 9:18 NKJV, "the needy shall not always be forgotten, the expectation of the poor shall not perish."

Every word of God is pure. He is a shield to those who put their trust in Him. "Charm is deceitful, and beauty is passing but a woman who fears the Lord she shall be praised," PROVERBS 31:30 NKJV. Learn how to love and not judge. Love with all your soul, be transparent and completely honest. God is mighty in strength and understanding, but he despises no one. It is more important to show your love through your actions. Give your life to God, and the Lord will provide. Jesus said, "Whatever I tell you in the dark, speak it in the light. Whoever confesses me before men, I will confess before my Father, who is in heaven," MATTHEW 10:27-29 NKJV.

Lord, help me hold on in this turbulent world, shine your light forward, and share your word with others. Let's give our praise at any time and moment and magnify God's Holy Name. Lord, I depend on you. PROVERBS 18: 20-21 NKJV tells us, "A man's stomach shall be satisfied from the fruit of his mouth; From the produce of his lips shall he be filled. Death and life are in the power of the tongue, and those who love it will eat its fruit." Lord, give me a clean mouth without toxic lips.

All of God's words matter. All our words matter. We must create things in our lives with the right words. Speak positively and affirm, "I declare and decree light is revelation." You receive what you believe. Our goal is to be full of the word of God. Hold onto the Word and use it when necessary. There is power in His unchanging Word, the commands that you have heard from the beginning. We walk in love, according to His commands. Worship is fellowship with God. "The path of the just is like the shining sun that shines even brighter," PROVERBS 4:18 KJV.

In MATTHEW 12:30 NKJV, the Lord says, "He who is not with me is against me, and he who doesn't gather with me is scattered abroad." My brothers and sisters, let every soul be subject unto the higher powers. There is no power but of God! The powers-that-be are ordained of God.

Lord, you formed man from the dust of the ground, breathed into his nostrils the breath of life, and we became living souls. We belong to you, and that is where we want to be, in the safe tower of your loving arms. Lord, I feel empty; fill me up with the river of living waters. Let your presence and love fulfill my soul. Pour your words and commands in my life. Let me walk in your testimonies and commands. My goodness is nothing apart from you. Fill me up until I overflow with your joy and peace. As for me, I want to see your face and righteousness. I will be satisfied when I awake in your likeness with a kingdom mindset in heaven. Thank you for your goodness, grace, mercy, and loving-kindness. I surrender to you. Amen.

Chapter 13

THE GIFT OF RIGHTEOUSNESS

"If anyone serves Me, let him follow Me; and where I am there, My servants will be also. If anyone serves Me, him My Father will honor," JOHN 12:26 NKJV. In all your ways, acknowledge Him, and He shall direct your paths. "Every branch in Me that does not bear fruit My Father takes away; and every branch that bears fruit He prunes that it may bear more fruit," JOHN 15:2 NKJV.

ISAIAH 26:9 NKJV states, "With my soul I have desired you in the night. Yes, by my spirit within me, I will seek you early; For when your judgments are in the earth, The inhabitants of the world will learn righteousness."

God gives us the gift of righteousness to enhance, strengthen, and make wiser our spiritual being. First, you receive salvation: deliverance from sin and its consequences. Your personal and in-depth relationship is a connection with our Creator. We have the freedom to choose to do what is right and just; most importantly, we receive eternal life to live with our Creator forever. Christians believe the gift of righteous conduct comes through faith in Christ. Worship is the attitude of our hearts, our thoughts, and our soul that thirst for God. Worship, our fellowship with God, is our key to pursue holiness and walk in authority with God.

We know that God has given Jesus all things in His hand and that Jesus came from God and went back to God, and now sits at His right-hand interceding on our behalf. Through one man's offense (Adam), judgment came to all men, resulting in condemnation for all humankind. Even so, through one man's righteous acts (Jesus), the gift of free will came to the human race, resulting in justification of life. Many became sinners by one man's disobedience, so many will be made righteous by one man's obedience. What the law could not do because it was weak through the flesh, God did by His own Son Jesus Christ in the likeness of sinful flesh on account of sin. Jesus condemned sin in the flesh so that the law's righteous requirements might be fulfilled in us who do not walk according to the flesh but of the spirit.

We love God and Lord Jesus: we know you are with us, Lord. Thank you for all you do for us. Marvelous are your mercies, and You are greatly to be praised. We must be on the battlefield in our full gear, walking with the sword of truth, covered with the breastplate of righteousness, shielded with the helmet of salvation, and proclaiming the word of truth. God is our oxygen: you do not see Him, but we always need Him. Worship Him forever -- not just during the good times. The Lord always covers His people coming in and going out.

Hallelujah, Hallelujah, I love to praise His Holy Name. God is so good it makes you just want to break out and sing praises to Him. The Lord loves those who love Him and diligently seek Him; He blesses those who walk in His ways. Jesus is the Christ, the divine Son of God. When you believe it, you have eternal life in His name. Hallelujah!

In JOHN 18:37 NKJV, we read, "Pilate, therefore, said to Him, 'Are you a king then?' Jesus answered, "You say rightly that I am a king. For this cause, I was born, and for this cause, I have come into the world that I should bear witness to the truth. Everyone who is of the truth hears My voice." Furthermore, in ACTS 1:8 NKJV, Jesus promises, "You shall receive power when the Holy Spirit has come upon you, and you shall be witness to Me in Jerusalem, and all Judea and Samaria, and to the end of the earth." We need to run to Jesus; Lord, turn us back to you, and we will be restored.

Obedience is the main staple in our walk with God. We must be obedient in all things pertaining to God. It is pure foolishness not to trust and obey the Lord, who has delivered us out of all our troubles. When trouble comes, people you thought were your friends disappear; they somehow forget who you are. Does this sound familiar?

Put your trust in Jesus because He is closer than any mother, brother, or sister. The Lord will never leave you; where He is there, you will be also. The Holy Spirit lives within us. Our God gives us His promises and His free-will gift of righteousness. All we must do is accept it and let Jesus be the center of our lives. There is one God and one mediator between God and men: Jesus Christ. Christ is divine and does not force anything on anyone; he gives you a choice to receive him if you choose. Salvation is one request away; ask Jesus our Lord to come into your life. Then watch and observe the gift of righteousness with all the blessings that the Father authorized Jesus to oversee. May the peace of God rest over your head and in your heart always. Amen!

Chapter 14

WHO ARE YOU IN CHRIST?

Who are you in Christ? What does this mean to you when you think about who you are? Are you examining yourself to find out? Are you spiritually engaged? For that matter, what does it take to be spiritually engaged? These are the vital questions you must ask yourself.

Consider the following three mandatory aspects of spiritual engagement:

1. Submission - to submit means to accept or yield to a superior authority or will of another person. In this case, it is obedience to God's will.

2. Surrender - to surrender means to cease resistance and submit to authority. In this case, God's laws.

3. Humility - to be humble means to possess modest or low esteem of one's importance, not proud, not self-assertive.

Becoming spiritually engaged begins with reading and believing in the Word. Next, we must pray about the Word and converse with God. When you talk to God, you are spiritually engaged. God is a spirit, and we worship Him in spirit and truth. Worshipping in spirit and truth means we must come clean; lying is not an option. If you are going to lie, do not bother talking to God because He will not answer you. When you come in truth, you are connected and committed to changing your way of thinking. By walking in the Word, you are obedient to it. When we submit and surrender ourselves, laying all our burdens on God, we become SAVED, LIVING, and FORGIVEN. Seek the Lord with all your heart.

Let me ask again: Who are you in Christ? Are you a Sunday saint or an everyday saint? There is a difference. You must be about God's business every day -- all day! You cannot sing and praise God's name on Sunday, then on Monday, do Satan's work. Please, Beloved, do not be a lost sheep in the House of the Lord. Do not straddle the fence; in other words, do not be wishy-washy. We must serve with a purpose to renew our minds daily and, in the process, help our brothers and sisters to be spiritually engaged. With your mind and heart, submit and surrender yourself, humble yourself, give your heart to God, and ask him to guide you with the Holy Spirit so you can serve Him with a pure heart.

Now, your prayer of submission can be as simple as the following: "Our Father's will be done; the will of God be done in my life, as it is in heaven. Teach me to do your will; you are my God. Let your Spirit lead me in the land of righteousness so that I can do the good and acceptable will of God. In Jesus' name, I pray. Amen."

God accepts your surrender. He is the fountain of life and the only source of existence, power, and glory throughout the universe. Have courage, and he will strengthen your heart and the hearts of all who hope in the Lord. When we follow Jesus, we imitate His way of living; His favor is on the faithful for life. PSALM 27:4 NKJV declares, "One thing I have desired of the Lord that I will seek: That I may dwell in the house of the Lord all the days of my life, To behold the beauty of the Lord, and inquire in His temple."

This scripture has a vast meaning. It teaches you to seek the Lord by communicating with Him. In doing so, you can truly find out who you are in Christ and what type of relationship you want to have with God. The blessing of God comes to those who seek Him with a pure heart. You can do it by confessing your wrongdoing and forgiving everyone. Make a sincere effort to change yourself to be obedient to his words. We can approach the throne of grace with confidence when we know our prayers move God. You have permission to pray for your own heart. Praying for God's divine order in our lives changes everything. HEBREWS 2:16 NKJV declares, "He does not give aid to angels, but He does give aid to the seed of Abraham," of which we are a part. When we pray, we are planting our seeds. When you put your seeds in the ground, what do you do next? You water them. By continuing to pray and be obedient to the Word, your harvest grows. Your answers to your prayers are coming to light where you recognize them and see that God is moving on your behalf -- it is not "good luck" -- it is God! PSALM 103:2-4 NKJV states:

> "Bless the Lord, O my soul,
>
> And forget not all His benefits:
>
> Who forgives all your iniquities (sins),
>
> Who heals all your diseases,
>
> Who redeems your life from destruction,
>
> Who crowns you with loving-kindness and tender mercies."

You might ask, "Are there going to be trying times after I give my life to Christ?" YES, without a doubt. God did not promise us sunshine, and there will be storms in your life. But if you endure, your reward will be exceptional. Do not waver in your faith. The Bible gives you the ability to live life skillfully. To seek God is to search the scriptures you have read; when we speak the Word, it is from the Bible.

If you did not already know, everything you need to know about life is on the pages of the Bible. If we live, we live for the Lord, and if we die, we die for the Lord; whether we live or die, we belong to the Lord. Take the Lord with you everywhere you go. Speak the word and claim your destiny.

Knowing who you are in Christ is a lifelong journey. We might fall down several times, but we must keep getting back up and align our hearts with

God's Word. We must stay connected, be spiritually engaged, submit, and surrender to the will of God. Humble yourself. We have authority in Christ Jesus; no weapon formed against us will prosper. We got the victory, claim it. God bless you all.

OBEDIENCE

The Key to Experiencing the Blessings of God at a Greater Level

Chapter 15

SEEK THE LORD

"There is one Lord, one faith, one baptism," EPHESIANS 4:5 NKJV. "In God is my salvation and my glory. The rock of my strength and my refuge is in God," PSALMS 62:7 NKJV. Trust in Him always, God's people, and pour out your heart before Him. God is our refuge.

ROMANS 8:1-2 NIV says: "There is no condemnation for those who are in Christ Jesus because through Christ Jesus the law of the spirit who gives life has set you free from the law of sin and death." To be spiritually minded is life and peace, and the spirit is life because of righteousness.

We are saved by HOPE, but hope is not seen. So why does man hope for it? If we hope for what we do not see, then we wait for it with patience. "We know that all things work together for good to those that love God; to them who are called according to His purpose," ROMANS 8:28 NKJV.

What shall I say to these things?

"If God is for us, who can be against us?" ROMANS 8:31 NKJV. It is God who justifies because His lovingkindness is better than life. Faith comes by hearing the word of God.

ROMANS 12:1-2 NIV says, " Therefore, I urge you, brothers and sisters, in view of God's mercy, to offer your bodies as a living sacrifice, holy and pleasing to God – this is your true and proper worship. Do not conform to the pattern of this world but be transformed by the renewing of your mind. Then you will be able to test and approve what God's will is—his good, pleasing and perfect will."

Let every soul be subject to higher powers. There is no power, but of God; the powers-that-be are ordained of God. "The night is nearly over; the day is almost here. So let us put aside the deeds of darkness and put on the armor of light… Jesus Christ," ROMANS 13:12 NIV.

Amen and Amen.

Chapter 16

GOD'S LOVE

You know faith began when God blew life into Adam, so righteousness and holiness kissed one another. Isn't that beautiful? Before the laws were written, we were righteous and holy in God's eyes. Bishop Joseph W. Walker III said, "You have to operate in the peace of God, to get your life in balance, to thank God for the storms in your life, because you are defined by your relationship in life, in God." God indeed is good; His loving-kindness is everlasting. One of the greatest gifts God has given us is His son, Jesus Christ. You can repent through Him by opening your mouth and acknowledging what you have done wrong with a sincere heart. God forgives us and washes our sins away — wow!

The Holy Spirit says, "Today if you hear His voice do not harden your heart as in the rebellion, in the days of trial in the wilderness," HEBREWS 3:7-8 NKJV. "Having now been justified by his blood, we shall be saved from the wrath of God through Him, that as sin reigned in death even so grace might reign through righteousness to eternal life through Jesus Christ our Lord," ROMANS 5:9,21 NKJV. "For this reason, I bow my knees to the Father of our Lord Jesus Christ, from whom the whole family in heaven and earth is named," EPHESIANS 3:14-15 NKJV.

Be watchful and refuse to continue to sin. Stop doing the same thing you know is wrong, repeatedly. You cannot continue to commit the same sin and think God will forgive you if you do not have a change of heart. It all falls under obedience; if you enter God's rest, you must be obedient. If you are disobedient, you shall not enter His rest. Please make no mistake about it; life is not a do-over. You have one life, and in your life, you must line up with God's words to receive your blessing. Therefore, many of us get ourselves into difficult situations, out of which we may not be able to escape.

My brothers and sisters, this is serious business! Our consequences are a result of our actions. Realign your heart, soul, and mind, and give your best to our Lord. He is abundant in mercy and grace. Keep it real, and be honest when you talk to our Father God. If you hear his voice, do not harden your heart. Come clean and stay clean. God is good, even when we are at our worst. "For *the death* that He died, He died to sin once for all; but *the life* that He lives, He lives to God," ROMANS 6:10 NKJV.

Chapter 17

CONSUMMATE YOUR LOVE FOR GOD

The dictionary defines consummate as "to make marriage or relationship complete, or perfect in every way; supreme; very skillful; highly accomplished." God is the consummation of all perfection. When you choose to have a relationship with Christ - who is the Church - you enter a marriage with Him. You have turned away from your sins and forsaken them; you have turned to God and placed your trust in Christ to lead you.

In JOHN 14:6,15 NKJV, Jesus says, "I am the way the truth and the life. No one comes to the Father except through Me. If you love Me, keep my commandments." And in JOHN 16:27 NKJV, "The Father Himself loves you because you have loved me and have believed that I came forth from God."

In PSALMS 16:3 NKJV, we read, "As for the saints who are on earth, 'they are the excellent ones in whom is all my delight.'" Jesus is the sanctuary minister and the true tabernacle which the Lord, *not* man, erected.

Do not think when you give someone a pass; it will not affect your salvation. We must tell both the sinner and righteous person when they err. Righteousness has no color; it is precisely right. Righteousness is God transformed in love; He delights in your righteousness. PROVERBS 11:30 NKJV tells us, "The fruit of the righteous is a tree of life, and he who wins souls is wise." Cleanse your conscience from dead works and serve the living God; death cannot be associated with the living God. God's gift is greater than our shame, His grace covers all our faults, and His greatness is unmatched. God reigns! God's inspiration is His love, kindness, benefits, and promises that meet all our needs.

Regardless of the situation you face, always trust the Lord, forever. Lord, let your word be magnified, and your Glory shine forward. We, as your children of light, must make quality time to study your Word and meditate in your presence. Wherever we walk, wherever we go, we will take the Lord with us. "As for me, I will see your face in righteousness; I will be satisfied when I awake in your likeness," PSALMS 17:15 NKJV. Lord, keep us as the apple of your eye; hide us under the shallow of your wings. We give you glory and praise Your Holy name. Hallelujah.

Chapter 18

FORGIVENESS

Some of us have our sight, yet we are blind to the teaching and ordinance of God. Take the time to remove the scales from your eyes, unplug your ears, most importantly, break the stone around your heart. Listen to and obey the Word God has given us to live by. Every day I will bless you, Lord, I will praise your name! Great is the Lord, and He is greatly to be praised; his greatness is unsearchable.

LUKE 24:48-49 NKJV states, "You are witnesses of these things. Behold, I send the Promise of My Father upon you; but stay in the city of Jerusalem until you are endued with power from on high." The Holy Spirit lives in us; it is one of the greatest gifts to mankind. We also have the power of prayer to commune with our God.

This is the message we have heard from Him and declare to you: God is light; in Him, there is no darkness at all. We have fellowship with Him, and we do not walk in darkness; we live in the truth. We walk in the light as He is in the light. We have fellowship with one another. The blood of Jesus, His Son, purifies us from sin.

"For the Father judges no one, but has committed all judgment to the Son, Jesus Christ, that all should honor the Son just as they honor the Father. Those that do not honor the Son do not honor the Father who sent Him," JOHN 5:22-23 NKJV. Jesus said, "This is the work of God, that you believe in Him whom He sent. The bread of God is he who came down from heaven and gives life to the world," JOHN 6:29,33 NKJV. Unless one is born again in the spirit, we cannot see the kingdom of God. We must all change our way of thinking and commit our lives to God. It is the only way to connect with Him! We cannot force the anointing, which must come from God, and is pure, not fake. The Lord will write his commands in your heart, it will be in your mouth, and you will speak the truth.

Bill Hybels said, "When our hearts are ruled by unresolved anger and conflict in relationships, the light of our witness begins to burn dimmer and dimmer. A breakdown of love is like a ruptured appendix." Forgiveness is our strength -- yes, we are stronger when we forgive if we are willing and obedient. Live your life purely in your action, as well as your mind. ISAIAH 3:10 NKJV tells us, "Say to the righteous that it shall be well with them, for they shall eat of the fruit of their doing." When we forgive people, it reveals our empowered spiritual gift; by doing so, they will see the glory we represent in the Lord.

How much favor, grace, mercy, and anointing does God give us? Is not forgiveness considered an unconditional love? Since the Lord of our salvation supplies us with this gift of love, should we not pray to remove the toxic thoughts in our mind and cleanse our conscience from dead and immoral works? The Lord sows into our lives daily; we must become inspired to share and sow into others the gift that God gave us. As I said earlier, forgiveness is our strength. We are stronger in God's eyes when we forgive and demonstrate love instead of hate or bitterness. God loves us unconditionally. We must also love unconditionally without respect for the person or group of people who despise us, hate us, and want to see harm come to us. It is difficult, but that is who we are. We represent the Kingdom of God and all His glory.

We are not perfect; we all fall short of glory. But remember this one thing: we are perfect in the Lord. His grace is sufficient for us. Therefore, let us march with integrity, not judging anyone, while we do the will of our Father walking in His grace. Amen.

SALVATION AND DEVOTION

A Clean Mind with an Open Heart

Chapter 19

CONFESSION

When you sin against God, you cannot hide; there are consequences to pay. How many times have you said, "I am not going to do this or that," and yet do it anyway? The flesh is battling against your spirit. It is warfare. You must pay the price for disobedience; only the blood of Jesus blocks out the Original Sin of Adam until the end of time. The goal is not to make you happy but to make you holy.

When you do not listen to God, you are bucking Him. That is the wrong place to be in because the consequences can be endless. However, God will forgive you! You must still pay the consequences; it is not pretty or enjoyable. It is easy for us to do wrong, but much harder to do what is right. We must be careful about the things we say and do. It is crucial to choose your words wisely. Do not speak out of anger; always strive to speak life and be positive. Every time you disobey God, you are piling coal on your own head; that's why God tells us it is a wicked and perverse world that hates Him. We are hard-headed and stiff-necked people. We think everything we do is right, but we are really messed up! The key point? We must stop trying to be right and, instead, endeavor to be righteous.

How do you become righteous? By walking in the will and understanding of God's Word. The Word is the seed of life, and our lifeline is trusting and having faith in the Word, the laws of God's covenant. Faith is the essential key to open the door so that God can come in. The only way He will listen to us is if we believe in Jesus Christ, whom He sent to save the world. No man can come to the Father except through the Son - the Light of the World who hanged on a tree, shed his blood on Calvary for the remission of our sins, and then rose on the third day. The blood of Jesus flows from the highest mountain to the lowest valley. It has the power to cleanse us, to heal us, and to take away the pain and suffering. It will never lose its power. When the blood covers you, it saves you and makes you whole. Nothing but the blood of Jesus can save you. You must believe, trust, and have faith. The result is Jesus has redeemed us back to His God and Father the Almighty, Holy, Omnipotence, Majesty, I Am that I Am, King of Kings, Jehovah.

Thank you, Lord, for loving me when I did not even love myself. Now I have a renewed mind and the right spirit within me. Father-God, forgive me when I do wrong unwillingly and give me a repenting heart. Lord, show me how to walk in your righteousness. Let me walk with integrity while keeping my mind and heart on you, doing what is right to please you, Lord. I need you, Father, I need your Holy Spirit to guide me in all things, to keep me on the path of righteousness all the days of my life. I respectfully ask in the Lord Jesus' name Amen.

Chapter 20

BE COMPLETE

ISAIAH 41:10 NKJV says, "Fear not for I am with you; Be not dismayed, for I am your God. I will strengthen you, Yes I will help you, I will uphold you with my righteous right hand." And ISAIAH 33:22 NKJV reminds us, "The Lord is our judge, the Lord is our lawgiver, the Lord is our King, and He will save us."

Today, right now, in this present moment I want to be complete in you. Be my strength every morning Lord. Help me to make good decisions and remove my personal feelings so that I can make the right decisions. Father God, your Word promises us in PROVERBS 21:21 NKJV that, "A person who follows righteousness and mercy finds life, righteousness, and honor."

Lord, I want to be complete and focus. I am all in for you. Let me walk in your perfect peace Father. Let me be a vessel of righteousness to walk in your integrity and let everyone see your righteousness in me Lord. Let them see your awesome power so then they will have a sincere heart to seek you, to learn your laws and promises. Then, Lord, they can build a relationship with You, the Highest God and Creator of the heavens and earth. These things I humbly ask in the Lord Jesus' name, Amen. Hallelujah.

Chapter 21

REVEALING THOUGHTS

You can never win if your attitude is off balance. Run your race and keep winning. Stand in the faith without fear. "There is no fear in love; but perfect love casts out fear because fear involves punishment and the one who fears is not perfected in love," 1 JOHN 4:18 NIV.

We go through different seasons in our lives, and with each season comes another lesson. A key point in learning is to remember your lessons from the past. It is like thinking back over your life and realizing how amazing the Lord our God has been to you. If you write or journal events, go back and reread them. You will recognize that many of the things you learned you stop using or visualizing in your mind to keep you sharp.

The same principle applies to reading the Bible. You cannot just read it one time and think you have absorbed the full context of its meaning. If you read it over and over, you will discover things you missed the first time that add value to your walk with Christ. The Bible is your spiritual food. I am hungry. I must read and eat the word always; I cannot get enough because the more I read, the more I learn. It takes me to a place where I experience spiritual fullness in my relationship with our Creator, God the Father. I never thought of it in that way, but it is so true. As Christians and God-fearing people, we must always continue to pour God's words into our souls.

We must see God as an elevator that raises us up. You must be at your best and cultivate a righteous mind instead of a sinful conscience. All these things add to the cause that we must seek God and obey His words. Live life in harmony with His commandments. In other words, you cannot be a 50% Christian. It is all in or nothing.

I pray God gives you the understanding I am trying to reveal to you; that as a working church, the most oversized room in your house (your temple) is the room for improvement. None of us have arrived; we must continuously improve and elevate our position to choose a closer relationship with God. God can only take you to where you are willing to go. Bishop Joseph W. Walker III said it best, "God can only take you where you are willing to go; God will bless you where God can take you." Do you want a kingdom relationship? If your answer is yes, elevate your mind to a deeper understanding of His words. God bless you all.

Chapter 22

PLANT YOUR SEED

Internal combustion is a buildup of pressure that can explode. In humans, a buildup of unresolved emotions can turn to rage and cause us to explode and hurt the people around us. Do not live your life in a state of constant combustion where minor issues cause you to blow a fuse. The critical point in your life is to trust God and believe in His words. When you establish an unwavering faith, all you ask for will be given to you. You have an anointing from the Holy One, and you know the truth. All who do the will of God abide forever.

"Lord, with your enduring patience, do not take it away; know that for your sake, I have suffered rebuke. Your words were found, and I ate them. Your words to me were joy and caused my heart to rejoice. I am called by your name," JEREMIAH 15:15-16 NKJV. The name of the Lord is a strong tower that the righteous run to for safety. A man's discretion makes him slow to anger, and his glory is to overlook a transgression. When you follow righteousness and mercy, you will find justice and honor. All who love with the purity of heart and grace on their lips, the King will befriend. A real friend always loves you.

The Lord remembers. His covenant is forever, the words which He commanded for a thousand generations. He permitted no one to do us wrong, saying, "Do not touch My anointed ones and do no harm to my prophet," PSALMS 105: 8,14-15 NKJV. He guards the path of justice and preserves the way of His saints. "Beloved, we are the children of God. It has not yet been revealed what we shall be, but we know when He is revealed, we shall be like Him, for we shall see Him as He is. Everyone who has this hope in Him purifies themselves just as He is pure," 1 JOHN 3:2-3 NKJV.

Nothing is hidden that will not be revealed, nor has anything been kept secret that should not come to light. "We know that the Son of God has come and has given us an understanding, that we may know Him who is true. We are in him who is true, in His Son Jesus Christ. This is the true God and eternal life," 1 JOHN 5:20 NKJV.

Brothers and Sisters, stay focused, come to the light, and break through the darkness that hinders your soul. Water the seeds you have planted. Your prayers are a seed, and prayer is something anyone can do at any time, in any place. Let your meditation be sweet to the Lord. Pour your heart out and give thanks to our Lord for His goodness and His wonderful works to the children of men. Take all His words and engrave them on your heart. Let the redeemed of the Lord give all their praises to our CREATOR. Amen.

Chapter 23

CONSCIENCE CHECK

Does your belief about Jesus match what 1 John teaches about Him? What are you going to do when your heart condemns you? What have you learned about sin? These are questions you should ask yourself and sincerely contemplate daily. When you read 1 John, it teaches you in-depth about Jesus. It contains five chapters packed with knowledge every Christian needs to know. The second question is easy - you repent and listen to what the Holy Spirit is telling you to do (the right thing); stop going off track. Now concerning sin, you confess your sins to God, ask for forgiveness, and He will cleanse you from all unrighteousness.

Are you practicing sin or righteousness? "He who has an ear let him hear what the Spirit says to the churches. To whoever overcomes I will give to eat from the tree of life which is in the midst of the Paradise of God. Do not fear any of the things which you are about to suffer. Indeed, the devil is about to throw some of you in prison that you may be tested and will have tribulation. Be faithful until death, and I will give you the crown of life," REVELATIONS 2:7,10 NKJV.

Let the truth abide in your spirit. With the testing of your soul, knowing Jesus enhances your spiritual state and fellowship with Him and one another. Let the truth of Jesus Christ live in you; be obedient and faithful to His commandments. God will provide for you. God searches our minds and hearts, and He will give each of us according to our works. "Cast your burden upon the Lord, and He will sustain you, He will never allow the righteous to be shaken," PSALMS 55:22 NIV. Our Lord is Holy and True.

What is in hell that you want?

If you love being a part of this world that hates God, and if you do not change your unrighteous thinking, deeds, evil desires, lust, and immorality, then hell is your home. You must decide: what is important to you, Salvation or Damnation? What is special about being burned alive in a fire that cannot be put out, a place where you suffer for eternity? In the beginning, God made us in His image. We were Holy because He was Holy. God walked in the garden with Adam and Eve and had a personal relationship with them until they ate from the forbidden tree of knowledge. This is when sin entered the world and broke our relationship with God, who cannot have any part of sin. That's why He sent Jesus to redeem us back to Him by dying on the cross for our sins and rising on the third day. God also gave us the right to make choices. He never forces our hand; we have free will to choose Him by being righteous in all things. On the other hand, you can select Satan by doing evil and ungodly things. You are either on God's team or Satan's team -- that is it! You have the choice to have a Robe and Crown in Paradise where rivers of living water flow; or burn in the Lake of Fire and Brimstone where you will spend eternity suffering at the hands of Satan and his demons.

We all want the best of everything. Living with the Father, Lord Jesus Christ, and the Holy Spirit is the only choice I accept. I belong to God, and that is where I want to be. God is everything to me. I need Him. I am sure we all agree that being in the presence of the Highest God is Joy and peace of mind to our soul. Amen.

COMMITMENT

Can God Count on You?

Chapter 24

A LISTENING EAR BECOMES AN OBEDIENT HEART

Hearing is a physical ability, but listening is a skill – understanding the meaning behind the words. Listening is an essential part of effective communication. This is God. Our God forever will be our guide even to death. The Lord's counsel will stand. God will redeem my soul from the power of the grave. He shall receive me.

This is the day that the Lord has made. I will rejoice and be glad in it. Call upon the Lord in the day of trouble. He will deliver you, and you shall glorify Him. God will be with your mouth and teach you what to say. God is not the God of the dead but the living. If we have God, we have everything we need. There is no need to worry; heaven will make our battle scars on earth worth it many times over. Stand firm and smile, knowing that great is your reward in heaven.

Commitment to God is developing a more profound devotion to Christ. You must create a heart of faith, a standard you apply in your spiritual life. Are you dependable? Can God count on you to be a soldier in His army? We must learn how to be trustworthy and determined to serve with a purpose to give our best. Yes, our best to be all in for Jesus, Father, Jehovah, I am that I am.

Uniting and growing in the Lord is our primary goal. We need Jesus to be the center of our lives. Everything we have is because of the blessing and grace of the Lord. I belong to you, Lord, and everything I have is yours. I give all my praise and worship to you, Father God. The Lord is our strength, and He is the saving grace of His anointed. Take up your cross daily and follow Jesus. If you will not do the work and cultivate your soul, how can your seed grow? A simple principle: if you do not work or put effort into salvation, how can you eat the crops' fruit? Come home to the Lord.

PSALM 57:2 NKJV says, "I will cry out to God the Most High, to God who performs all things for me." If you faint in the day of adversity, your strength (faith) is small. Be ready always; do not be afraid to say yes to God, yes to faith. Father, take the hardness from around my heart, give me a repentant heart, a clean heart to walk in your statutes, to do your will.

As a nation of believers, we cannot afford to walk in our understanding. We must align all our hopes and desires to serve the Lord by walking faithfully in the anointing He has placed on our lives. We must know what it means to be committed to Jesus Christ. Let the anointing overflow in our lives as we become true imitators of Christ, loving one another as Jesus loved us. We will not take anything for granted except the love of God poured out on us from heaven above. We will be diligent in our prayers, supplications, and devotion to you, Lord. We thank you continually and honor your Holy name.

Our resources are the Holy Bible, which we will study to learn how to walk each day. We will live each day as if we are in the resurrection in heaven with You right now in this present moment and time. Everywhere we go, we will be in Your presence Lord. As Your people, we must change our ways and walk with a kingdom mindset. Our minds must be on a higher elevation, aligned with God's word for our life. A Godly purpose can never be destroyed. Live your life for the one who can save you - God's Son, Jesus Christ.

"The refining pot purges the impurities out of silver and the furnace for gold, but the Lord tests the hearts," PROVERBS 17:3 NKJV. Let us consider ourselves in the refining pot that God is purging us to be Holy as He is Holy. We strive to sit at the right side of the Lord to gain access to the kingdom of eternal life. Chosen and faithful through God, we will do valiantly, for it is He who shall tread down our enemies. Listen to the Lord's counsel, and He will fill your days with His love, joy, and collected treasures. What God has blessed is blessed forever. Amen.

Chapter 25

TRANSFORMED INTO THE LIGHT

LUKE 16:10 NKJV tells us, "Whoever can be trusted with very little can also be trusted with much, and whoever is dishonest with very little will also be dishonest with much." God builds all things. If God is not in it, the labor is in vain.

Do not let your mouth lead you into sin. How can a person stay on the path of a righteous life? By living according to God's word, to seek Him with their whole heart, and not stray from His commands. Lord, your judgments are right, and in faithfulness, you have afflicted me. Your merciful kindness comforts me according to your promise to your servants. Everyone whom God has given wealth and the ability to enjoy them is the gift of God. Let every soul transform into the light.

The word is the only thing that cannot be taken from you. Blessed are those who hear the word of God and keep it. This is the focal point to understand Jesus' message. Once Jesus touches and transforms our hearts, we inherit His heart and become righteous. We cannot meet His high standard in our own righteousness, but we can inherit His righteousness. Lord, direct our steps by your word and let no iniquity have dominion over us. PSALM 37:23,25 NKJV says, "The Lord makes firm the steps of the one who delights in Him. I was young, and now I am old, yet I have never seen the righteous forsaken or their children begging bread." God takes care of His people.

The essence of Christianity is when people offer their full hearts to worship God. When you give everything to God in worship, things change for your betterment. You are committed to doing good for others to show how a person should love everyone, walk in the way of your heart, and the sight of your eyes, knowing God will bring this into judgment.

Dr. Douglas L Robinson Jr. said, "As we grow in our Christian walk, worship must become a lifestyle, rather than an activity for church only. The declaration of Holy, Holy, Holy, reinforces our actions to be upright and reflects a Christ-centric dedication. This suggests that our neighbors are observing whether our words mirror our steps. If we appear hypocritical, we nullify our witness of Christ. However, if we stand committed to practicing what we profess with our mouth, we will win souls to Christ. The power of Christ living inside of us triggers a transformation that awakens the world to ask the question: what is it about you that makes you so different? Then we can begin to express how Jesus changed us."

Only God can put words of wisdom in a man's mouth to speak His truth! Make no mistake, to be transformed into the light, you must line up God's word to receive your blessing. Life is not a game you can play again, but you can adjust and realign your faith to walk with God. Your reality can change your position and give you a new life as a spiritual disciple of Jesus. Consider what you are doing; God will not have any part in anything that is unrighteous.

God, you are good, and your mercy endures forever. We are servants and soldiers of God. We must go through the training to enable us to wear the whole armor of God. Standing on the Word helps us to fight off the attacks the enemy has thrown at us and come out victorious in Jesus' name. I am walking in the authority God gave me. I am using it to transform into the light.

Forever, "Let your light so shine before men that they may see your good works and glorify your Father in heaven," MATTHEW 5:16 NKJV. Family, we must have an all-hands-on-deck attitude, always guarding our post and conducting ourselves in a manner that pleases God. Let us boldly walk with one mind and one mouth glorifying our God in His righteous truth and let His will be done. We are His Saints transformed into the light; do not let your oil burn out: refill it and stay strong. Amen.

Chapter 26

PURIFIED IN THE LIGHT

GALATIANS 2:20 NKJV says, "I have been crucified with Christ; it is no longer I who live, but Christ lives in me, and the life which I now live in the flesh I live by faith in the Son of God." Pure is defined as "free from defects, perfect, faultless, free from sin or guilt, blameless." Light is defined as bright, something that makes things visible or affords illumination.

By following Christ's example of extending grace and mercy to others, we will be reminded of Christ's light, and it will shine from us. We will walk worthy of the God who calls us into His kingdom and glory; for this reason, we thank God without ceasing. Everyone wants the blessing of the Lord Jesus when we seek His presence. We ask for favor, prosperity, grace, a long life, etc. Then we resist doing what the Lord asks of us because it is uncomfortable. Like helping those in need and feeding and clothing the homeless. It became a big deal because we have gotten puffed up or feel entitled. What is wrong with this picture?

A servant who serves must give the Lord His just due. We always want God to give and bless us when we ask Him. In return, how much time do we give God in service by serving Him with a pure heart -- not complaining or being resentful because we do not feel like it or want to do it? We want everything without putting in the work. Our priorities are backward. It is all about me, me, me. Where is the love, where is the desire to walk in the light, purified? We are God's creation, His workmanship, and His masterpiece. His glory is revealed in us as we live like Him and do as He instructs us.

He has called us to do His good works, reflecting the nature of Jesus Christ within us. It was God's plan from the beginning. We all want God to bless us, so when God blesses us, we must serve him and be a blessing to someone else to be purified in the light. Live the word by walking in the word.

To imitate Jesus and do the Father's will, we cannot hold grudges or say, "I forgive you, but I will not forget." If these words are in your heart, have you *truly* forgiven the person? I say no because you have resentment in your heart. Why do we forgive our enemies? In a word, Jesus. His sacrifice to save us, knowing we were all born in sin. Jesus came down to earth from heaven, took off His robe and crown, and laid down His life for us freely for our sake that we may have eternal life. That is not only love. It is agape love, beyond the understanding of our mind. He did not say, "I forgive you, but I will not forget." His words were, "Father, forgive them, for they know not what they do."

In the book of Matthew, Peter asks Jesus, "How many times must I forgive my brother, seven times?" Jesus replies, "Seven times seventy, 490 times a day." The point Jesus was making is that every time a person sins against you and repents their sins, you must forgive them.

PROVERBS 18:4 NIV says, "The words of the mouth are deep waters, but the fountain of wisdom is a rushing stream." 1 CORINTHIANS 15:22-23 NIV declares, "As in Adam all die, so in Christ, all will be made alive. But each in turn: Christ, the first fruits, then when he comes, those who belong to Him." What is the importance of these scriptures? First, God gives us wisdom and understanding to discern His word in our daily life. Second, Christ is the first person of the resurrection, never to die again. This is everlasting life.

Beloved, what God has for you, no man can take away. Do not get discouraged when people hate you without a cause. Watch and stand fast in the faith, be brave and strong. Let your speech always be with grace, seasoned with salt, so you may know how you ought to answer each person.

God is like oxygen; you do not see Him, but you need Him. There is not a friend like Jesus, no not one. Jesus knows all about our troubles, and He will abide until the day is done. You cannot control what happens to you, but you can control how you respond. "The things that proceed out of your mouth come from your heart, and those things can defile a man," notes MATTHEW 15:18 NKJV. Purify yourselves in the light. When the spirit of the Lord is on you, your enemies are afraid of you. They act as if they are your friend, but they devise wickedness and evil deeds toward you in their hearts. Stay grounded and keep your focus on the Lord. He will deliver you out of all your troubles when you are hurting or in a painful situation; go to the rock, your foundation where you stand, or lay face down and call on the name of Jesus. Get purified in the light.

PROVERBS 22:4,6 NIV clearly states, "Humility is the fear of the Lord; its wages are riches and honor and life," and Verse 6 says, "Start children off on the way they should go, and even when they are old they will not turn from it." 2 CORINTHIANS 1:3-4 NIV states, "Praise be to the God and Father of our Lord Jesus Christ, the Father of compassion and the God of all comfort, who comforts us in all our troubles so that we can comfort those in any trouble with the comfort we receive from God." Walk in the light, "Through love and faithfulness sin is atoned for; through the fear of the Lord, evil is avoided," PROVERBS 16:6 NIV.

God will destroy His enemies and bring unparalleled blessings to those who faithfully obey Him. The keyword is obedience. Yahweh is God: let all things be done for edification, you can all prophesy one by one, that all may learn and be encouraged. Let all things be done decently and in order. Let no one cheat you out of your reward. Set your mind on things above and remember the substance of Christ. COLOSSIANS 3:1 NIV reminds us, "Since then, you have been raised with Christ, set your hearts on things above, where Christ is, seated at the right hand of God."

If we love the Lord God, we will do His will. First, say to yourself, "I must forget the things I think in my mind. Second, I must stop worrying about being right." We renew ourselves by being righteous instead of being right. We must let the Holy Spirit guide us. Realize our thoughts are not God's thoughts. Let go, walk in the Spirit and come before the presence of the throne of grace with an open and clean heart, seeking the anointing our God has for us.

His yoke is not hard. We make it hard because of our thoughts and the way we reason. His yoke is easy. God's yoke is binding us together with Him. Do not contemplate; just do what is right and follow your heart, the heart God gave you to do all things decently and in order. Take his word and absorb it like water in a sponge. Free yourself from the cares of this world, refresh yourself, and walk in holiness. Thank you, Jesus, for being the light that shows us the way to follow.

Purify your mind, call on the name of Jesus watch things open in your favor. Jesus' name has power. He opens doors that need to be opened and closes doors that need to be shut. If he opens a door, no one can shut it. If He closes a door, no one can open it. We need Jesus in our lives. Do not get left behind. Where Jesus is, that is where we should be. We died with him, and we will be raised with him. JOHN 14:27 NIV Jesus declares, "Peace I leave with you; my peace I give you. I do not give to you as the world gives. Do not let your hearts be troubled and do not be afraid."

God's people, let us talk the talk and walk the walk. Follow Jesus, the Son of God, our Messiah, our Savior, our God, our Lord, and everything. Be purified in the light. Jesus is the light. All who call on Jesus, change your ways, refresh your soul, walk into the marvelous light, let justice run down your soul like water, and righteousness like a mighty stream. Be purified in the light of God's Son, Jesus. Amen…Hallelujah.

Chapter 27

CLOSING THOUGHTS AND PRAYER

ISAIAH 58:11 NKJV says, "The Lord will guide you continually, And satisfy your soul in drought, And strengthen your bones; You shall be like a watered garden, And like a spring of water, whose waters do not fail."

Have you ever noticed in the morning before the sun comes up how the birds start singing? It dawned on me that the birds were giving God praise to thank Him for another day. If the birds can give God glory every day, shouldn't we do the same? The Lord has blessed us far more. When I am studying or doing devotion early, and I hear the birds singing, it gives me joy, knowing I am not the only one praising our Creator at that time. If only to say, "Thank you, Father, for all you have done for me, thank you for loving me, I am grateful You are in my life." God does not ask for much, just for us to acknowledge Him and treat each other with love. Take the time to tell God how much you appreciate Him.

Reverence is defined as "a feeling or attitude of deep respect, love tinged with awe, a gesture indicative of deep respect, an obeisance, bow, or curtsy for something sacred." In modern times, it is often used in relationship with religion. This is because religion often stimulates emotion through the recognition of God, the supernatural. When you hear the term "Fear the Lord," what does it mean? It does not mean to be afraid of God but to give reverence to God by following His laws and commands to live a righteous life and be aware that He watches everything you do; He knows everything.

Make me new, Lord, plant in me the heart of Jesus and let His righteous ways shine forth so all can see the glory of the Lord. We are the children of royalty. Let our array of light shine boldly into the atmosphere. I am not ashamed to call on your name. I embrace your presence every day with joy in my heart. Our citizenship is in heaven, where we eagerly await our Savior, the Lord Jesus Christ.

Lord, prune me take away all my iniquities, purify my soul, and wash me clean as snow. Let me come before your presence obediently, let my obedience be considered holiness, and please you, Lord. I need you. Everything I am is because of your great mercies, Lord. Thank you, Father, for covering and protecting me; Father, your word says, those who get wisdom love their souls, and whoever keeps understanding will find goodness. Father God, you are my goodness and my friend. I lift my hands to bless your holy name.

My brother once told me to "embrace every change of my life in a positive light. Never be fooled to think that change means God has left your side. He will always uphold you with His right hand." There is a blessing in your life. Stand under the fountain of living water and let the Lord pour into you. Your destiny is tied to your everyday choices; we have power given to us by God; do not give it away on useless idolatry. Use it to save a soul or to lift one in need.

Let this generation be known as the one that did their best. Your fire burns within our hearts, Lord. We desire to live out your will to be full of the gospel. We raise our hands and speak your truth. We worship You and give You our best. You are God Almighty, and You are good. We will tell our story and give you, God, all the glory.

"No weapon formed against you shall prosper, and every tongue which rises against you in judgment you shall condemn. This is the heritage of the servants of the Lord, and their righteousness is from Me, says the Lord," ISAIAH 54:17 NKJV. Patience is a virtue. We all must learn how to be patient; rushing blindly into things does not produce the outcome we may want. Trusting in the Lord is patience because you know God will deliver on His word. His promises have been ever-present in our lives. When you let God move on your behalf, there is nothing you will lack or need. Submit to the will of the Father, the promises will come, and waiting will pay off. Be patient, and the peace of God will bless your life.

I pray and hope these words have enlightened you to press forward and have given you the desire to serve the Lord with your whole heart and your total being without compromise. God bless and keep you.

Stay prayerful!

About the Author

Illinois native Lamont Hill has been writing since he was young. A graduate of Thornton High School, United Technical Institute, Wilberforce University, and Southern Illinois University, Hill spent 25 years in the trucking industry and retired from YRC Trucking in 2007.

An active participant in the Prison Ministry, Hill's passion is to uplift people from all walks of life. He strives to reach those who do not believe in God so that they may receive the inheritance of God's Kingdom; excel and achieve their goals in life; and help others that cross their paths to be better human beings.

In his spare time, Hill loves to read, travel the world to experience new cultures, play chess, do yard work, and cook. He currently resides in Tennessee with his wife, Shirley.

References

New International Bible
www.BibleGateway.com/versions/New-International-Version-NIV-Bible/

The Bible - New King James Version
www.BibleGateway.com/versions/New-King-James-Version-NKJV-Bible/

Amplified Bible

https://www.biblegateway.com/versions/Amplified-Bible-AMP/

Breaking the Curse From a Twisted Life: Bad Habits, Addictions, and the Generational Curse, Frank Turner, Jr.
Amazon.com/Breaking-Curse-Twisted-Life-Generational/dp/1449716385

Frances Taylor Gench
www.upsem.edu/about/faculty/frances-taylor-gench/

Dr. Douglas L. Robinson
www.mmc.edu/_modules/news/robinson_story.html

Bishop Joseph W. Walker III
www.JosephWalker3.org/

Mt. Zion Baptist Church
Elder Mary Dalton
Elder Opal Scales
James Davis
www.mtzionnashville.org/ministries

Bill Hybels
Amazon.com/Bill-Hybels/e/B000AQ4QPO%3Fref=dbs_a_mng_rwt_scns_share

MY JOURNEY WITH THE LORD

NOTES TO HELP YOU STAY CONNECTED

Notes On My Personal Journey With The Lord

www.ingramcontent.com/pod-product-compliance
Lightning Source LLC
Chambersburg PA
CBHW071715040426
42446CB00011B/2081